THE CASK
OF MOONLIGHT

First published in 2014 by
The Dedalus Press
13 Moyclare Road
Baldoyle
Dublin 13
Ireland

www.dedaluspress.com

ISBN 978 1 906614 95 9

Dedalus Press titles are represented in the UK by
Central Books, 99 Wallis Road, London E9 5LN
and in North America by Syracuse University Press, Inc.,
621 Skytop Road, Suite 110, Syracuse, New York 13244.

Printed in Dublin by Gemini International Ltd.

Cover image © Dinozzaver | Dreamstime.com

The Dedalus Press receives financial assistance from
The Arts Council / An Chomhairle Ealaíon

THE CASK
OF MOONLIGHT

Patrick Kehoe

DEDALUS PRESS
DUBLIN, IRELAND

ACKNOWLEDGEMENTS

Thanks are due to the editors / publishers of the following in which a number of these poems originally appeared: *The Irish Times, Cyphers, Enniscorthy Echo,* and the anthologies *Red Lamp Black Piano* and *Dust Motes Dancing in the Sunbeams.*

Thanks to Pat Boran, Eamonn Wall, Billy Roche, Andrew Motion, Carl Corcoran, Sonny Condell, the late James Liddy, Paul Funge and Liam O'Connor.

Contents

☙

III

IV

֍

To Mary, Sorcha and Cormac

There's no new land, my friend, no
New sea; for the city will follow you,
In the same streets you'll wander endlessly ...

— 'The City', Constantine Cavafy

A Welcome Here

A welcome here, after hard times,
Key to the door, a bed in the corner.

Morning inviolate with light,
The city stretching down to the harbour.

These terra firma streets inscrutable,
Barely known, below the traffic noise;

You too would come, fresh flower,
Evanescent, fall of water on parched sand.

Swim Without Thinking

Today the hard jewel of the city
Looked at you as a woman
Might stare, then revert to type.

The alien sun in its vacant lot,
Oily suburbs, filthy sidings;
Years on, you have yet to

Swim without thinking
Under the trees' expansive rustle,
The way they woo the afternoon

And whisper in the breeze.

Argentina

Two guys from Argentina
Talking away that first night,
I slept on a mattress on the floor

Unable to understand a thing;
Spain, a word come into its own
Like it or not, being there was stumbling

Into the wardrobe of another's dream.
I read the signs through the heat haze,
Instructions involved a street named

Calle de La República de Argentina,
Then Argentina won the World Cup;
I prized a living out of the livid city.

Dawn Draining, 1979

Dawn draining from the streets,
And the clouds of fog hovering
Above the harbour front.

The candleabra melting,
One entire night of staying up
With new-found friends,
Just as soon forgotten.

Long for nothing,
Stop the search:
All is shadow, ghost land.

Vibrant Grey Light

Si dolce è'l tormento
Ch'in seno mi sta,
Ch'io vivo contento
Per cruda beltà

I was not there long and the city said
Stay tonight, in a lost acre of streets
From whose map the blood has seeped.

Ramble in vibrant grey light, the city said;
The avenues opened their green palms
And would not let me forget.

Imagine the Rooms

Imagine the rooms,
Cumulus of piled light,
Our time in them, gone.

Starved dusk, people walking
To stations, past sweet-shops,
Heartless boutiques
In five o'clock shadows.

Imagine the rooms,
All who lived in them.

The Name of the City

Outages and outrages, and the wingbeat
Of what is over and done with
Clinging as the late butterfly
Clings to the callow August window.

Over and done with:
Even mention of the city's proud name
Is believed by common consent
To be blasphemy, frightening the stone horses.

Names

Alas, Amador, Belles, Llorens,
Names carved in stone by men
Who are themselves dust.

Calix, Grau, Mercer, Novella
Plume, Polit, Prior, Pujol
Quint, Revello, Torrens, Vidal:

A woman's eyes a man might
Drown in, but women
Coyly told the men

Their names, now cold
On marble mausoleums,
Now carved on grave stones.

Hands

Pure as the driven sun our hands,
In that transient domain of light.

Eta had bloody hands, they killed
100 people that year; tied the hands

Of victims; families walked, white-faced,
Death warmed up, Adolfo Suárez

Sat on his hands in the Palacio de la Moncloa
Brooding over cups of coffee,

Sleeping pills, amphetamines;
And pure as the driven sun, our hands.

What the Oud Knows

The oud, forerunner of the lute,
The lute itself, and their cousin
The guitarra Flamenca
Saw through your game.

The oud, heard behind blinds
Drawn on what is left unsaid,
Penumbral architect
Of secret explaining.

The oud, the lute
And the Flamenco guitar
Saw through your game
And did not stay silent.

Bar Zurich

Freeze frame and steel shutter,
Grey sheet of dawn hauled
Over the city's unwashed face.

Now that we have exhausted
Whatever nameless thing it was
That resembled love,

Linger in the cask of moonlight,
Seek out the lamp-lit church
Of Sant Felip Neri without consolation.

Nothing was intended,
There was to be no wide arc
Through the sky of the years

Save wet circles
From a beer glass
At Bar Zurich.

Two Women

PILAR

The early morning sweeper has been,
The street is gone, its absence like wormwood.

Her name in a bilious green notebook
Pilar Salvi, and her street Verge del Pilar.

Lamenting of the choirs,
Grandiose folly of remembering.

MARGA

Are you in the streets of Poble Sec
Or walking in Passeig de Gràcia?

The breeeze whispers your name
Under the incurious moon.

Your green eyes in Tuixent,
Rough roads, that winter day

In the Serra del Cadí.

Violent for Your Furs

Outside, the city
At its torrid affair
While night was telling us
To seize the day.

Now that there is room to think

And tidal dark
Wonders where to beach us,
Hands race around
The weary clock face.

In the Market of Sant Josep

Pyramids of oranges, ziggurats
Of passion fruit, glistening fishes,
Prime cuts, offal: market-sellers

Lost in their dreamscape
Of bargain banter, pinned
And pronged by talk.

Say no more, think no more,
Remember no more; dignity of waiters
In the bars on Calle Boqueria,

Night folds out another accordion,
All I never saw.

Walking Near La Floresta

Remember how the city cleared
Of its citizens, many of whom
Had gone to the mountains,
Hidden in castles of ash and pine.

Remember the fragrance
Of the eucalyptus tree,
Burnt Sunday afternoon shadows
Alive as light in a clearing.

You were once a stripling abroad,
Who did not know
That on the brightness of arrival
Already is falling the cloud of leave-taking.

April

April and its loud hailer
Did shout loudest about the season

Did step wildly upon
The debris of dead winter

Did walk with heavy tread
Igniting the plane trees.

Gold Leaf City

Float here, trembling heart
Recover the terra-cotta city:

The blues lies down
In reverie's windowseat.

Cinema once, there
In winter shadows

Where the streets level
After gradual rise

Beehive ways of the city
Where we walked.

Through the open shutters comes
Memory's sandy slattern breeze.

We emerged into the yellow light
Of evening and stood transfixed,

Walked into gold leaf city,
Down Ronda de San Antonio

Saturday's free hours
Before the evening crystallised:

Nothing to write home about
But everything to live for.

Plaza Molina, breath of summer wind
Desert grains in the doorway.

This was long ago,
Long before the sifting of the hour glass.

Dissabte

A sudden gust of cigar smoke —
Self-raising, quick-flowering rose

Of tobacco from the man
In the car coat on Calle Pelayo —

Says all is well in this place
Where Gothic bell towers

Have sounded through sleeping centuries;
Saturday, Dissabte —

Imploding in the memory vault.

In the Amber Hush of Dusk

In an upstairs room we once saw
Through an open window,
How April combed soft tresses of light.

Now, in the amber hush of dusk
The street remembers
But the winter trees are silent;

Only bandoneon music,
And Adriana Varela singing *las mujeres*
Siempre son las que matan la ilusión.

To awaken again in Barrio Gótico
In the shadow of La Catedral,
In la Plaça de la Seu.

Calle Provenza

Our failed cadenza
Was nothing new under the sun,
Glass-blown light falling
On the patios and balconies of Calle Provenza.

All for the singing of a bossa nova song
A few gilded guitar chords,
Distractions of memory
In a fey, early morning light.

Hour of the Siesta

You and I knew each other
When a street emptied in the afternoon

And the plane trees were awake in green
To the new spill of light.

Years have passed, hour of the siesta,
Not a stray leaf left.

The avenues are pools of black water,
Shaded streets that shiver with memory.

Persianas

Once we were two
But one among our friends,
They said our names
In bars and public places.

Brassy blossom falling,
We were awake in the cirrus and blue,
Or whirring through the underground
From the dance at La Paloma

The night in Santa Maria del Mar.
Now green shutters at the windows
Are open on the day,
The diffident tree obscures

What used to be my room;
A few leaves on its branches,
As if to say 'not ready yet'
Or 'that was a long time ago.'

Women of La Mancha

The three women of La Mancha
On their paseo, were startled
By what they saw.

You came breathless
From a different hemisphere:

The three women of La Mancha
Stopped to look, before walking onward
With corruscating grace.

When Spring Comes

When spring comes
With its streams and whispers
Violets on the make, taffeta jazz,

I will see again flaxen hair,
Eyes of cornflower blue
In chiaroscuro streets

In charcoal shadows;
When spring comes
With its streams and whispers.

Miles to Hear Before I Sleep

Our eyes met, wavered as water disturbed
Then fixed darkly, hunter and hunted;

The powder blue stage whisper
Sifting from the dome of the sky.

Remember the night we walked home
Along the street named after Enrique Granados

Brass and reed folded away in velvet,
The kindly hair-oiled musicians

Gone to bed; time for us to lay
Our tired heads in the Nubian night.

Better sometimes the song without words,
Persian blue sky breathless with falling stars

Above the city roofs, the brass funicular of jazz
Crawling celestial out of the earth.

Avenida Diagonal i

The woman in the pomp
Of her spendthrift days
Cast the white ardour of surf
Upon you as she hit the sand.

And after, the solo walk across the desert
Of Avenida Diagonal, caught between
The sweltering cars and the faithless sunlight.

The Deserted Beaches

As praias desertas continuam
Esperando por nos dois

The deserted beaches are waiting
But we will not return at dawn or dusk;
The street where you lived

Is a river, it carries a cargo
Turned extraordinary through memory,
The worker in gold.

But winter, the consumptive waiter,
Cannot recall us, for we rose
Like sap in a different season.

Canaletas, the Fountain

Once there was light slipping
Along a wall at evening, a name
In a book, a number on a door.

Vast city, and Canaletas, the fountain;
It was said that the one who drank
From its waters would never leave.

And we have not left, our migrant love
Fallen down the years upon the wind
Into the chamber of a Brazilian song.

In rivulets of oblivion endures
What we had, when we flowered
Amongst the cacophony of the cars.

The Plaza at Vic

The Plaza at Vic
Is bathed in the blue milk of dusk
From which is cleared
All breath and swathe of us.

The train to Vic
Travelled along the track,
Night at the end of the journey,
Pale stars, the promise of eyes.

To search is to restore the dulled print
Of an old film, something nouvelle vague
That lingers, malingers
Like a fly in a storm screen.

Santa Maria del Mar

We stood outside the church
Of Santa Maria del Mar
Where we heard the Breton harper play;
He made magic from steel strings

He sang. Colour blessed us,
Its sheen over all things.
We walked to Via Laietana,
Long before this longer night

Impregnated black as shadows
Lost in now. I hear the tape twist
And reverse and the music of the harper
Like wind in a tunnel; then applause

Followed by the tunnel sound again.
The wind sings that colour blessed us
The beginning of our measures,
The dance of our lives.

The Judas Tree

The Judas Tree blooms in April,
Cercis Siliquastrum has pink flowers
Before the leaves appear.

We walked under lots of trees,
Beneath the Judas Tree
We might have paused

And stood in its shade;
But we were not there
For the bitter fruit

The dark brown pods
Which appear in autumn,
And remain through the winter.

Entradas

For a while the country was much as it had been; then,
climbing all the time, we crossed the top of a col, the road
winding back and forth on itself, and then it was really
Spain.
— Ernest Hemingway, *'Fiesta' (The Sun Also Rises)*

We came our different ways to the city,
You came later, I was already there

Came first to light rain outside the station
And wet trees on the Ramblas.

You must have come like the drum major sun
Or the loudest whisper of fountain water.

That month recalled by one or two at most,
Like tendrils of ivy that remember their tree host.

La Modelo

Anything might break out:
A man might ride a horse through a bonfire
In honour of Saint Anthony,
Or the tobacco laws come to nothing
In smoke-rings and evasion.

Here we lived once, indefatigable,
Unaware of the power within:
Look back and insist we were strong,
Though we were fragile as tears.

Across the street, the peeling walls
Of La Modelo prison, a guard
Smoking in his look-out tower; up close
In our single bed, beneath the crown of stars,
Shape of the plan already dissolving.

What We Burrowed Out of the Spring

A sun-blasted train along the coast,
Perfume of the pines: each heard
The other's song of yearning,
What we burrowed out of the spring.

Oak doors of the proud Catalan
In his fastness; now watchman
Will not wake, city dare not speak its name,
Street unlock, nor door open.

Moth-Like You Were

You were borrowed blue,
Iris stopping the transport
Of the street; seraphic, moth-like

Towards twilight, not a breeze
On the merciless bridge
Above the underpass.

On the inner arterial route
Only the deathless cars speeding;
Night river, warm bed.

The Rendezvous

Would it not have been better
Had I stopped on my way,

A roll of dice, an absinthe in that bar,
Or small talk with the friend I hurried past

Hoping he did not see me on my vaunted way,
The star-strewn path to our assignation.

Amphora

There is a maze of stalls
In the plaza by the church,
Memory of a rose
Held in a woman's hand

In the white blaze of noon.
Una Furtiva Lagrima
Heard through rattan blinds
In an open window.

A chair asks to speak,
A street bench cries:
This is the amphora,
What was carried.

Manhã de Carnaval

Among all torn flowers
This morning of the carnival;
Yesterday morning
We were yet to be.

Leave all talk of this city,
Depart on a cable car
Above the terra-cotta roofs;
Take your escape clause of the damned.

Indigo

Back he came, arriving by humid night
Stars like brass filings
Sailing granite façades,
A white cloud in the indigo sky.

Old cigar smoke, diners
At outside tables on Paseo de Gracia.

Begin to live here again, a thread
In the morning, pick up the pieces:
That room in the pensión,
Zig-zag pattern in the carpet.

Careless Love

All your tiresome jive
Leaves so much
Dead coffee grounds;
El Cigala is singing

Of love deep as a gorge
And Camarón too:
'*Quiero quitarme de esta pena.*'
Hear him on the nervy juke box

On the ordinary street
Of laughter and tears,
The ashtray with all
That has expired.

They sat together here once
Who walked alone afterwards,
To other places, singing
Of their careless love.

Calle Padilla

Pandemonium on Calle Padilla,
A man is fighting his Gothic dream shadows
Recently dissolved.

Will he go or will he stay?
He is back for a few frigorifically hot days,
As if the city was a healer.

The last place he should be
In fact, with its jeering birds
And relentless march of the thoughtless cars.

Back, in any case, to the pre-dream life,
Dastardly night lead sinker,
Slow creep day without her.

The city a tin box, and inside
The grids and bevelled angles
A man fighting, wild punches thrown.

Blue and Gold

Blue and gold you came:
I can reel it back again,
Not word for pale word
But in the fall of lamplight.

What were the clothes we wore
And what were the things we said?

Blue and gold you walked
Through the streets of Via Augusta,
Rosellón and Consejo de Ciento.

No One There on Return

No one there on return,
No one along the echoing colonnade;
Not a soul recognised at these tables

Where talk is like the clanging of keys
Locking a door that will not close;
In the fracas of the city, not one familiar face.

Sad air of the duduk, left trailing in our wake.

Feuille Morte

Their last kiss, a useless dead thing
September night, the vast city
Hot like cordite, a furnace

So hot winter could not be imagined;
Rumble of the wind in lift shafts, vents,
Window frames, door jambs

Breaths like ice clouds.

Sant Felip Neri

Sunday evening blackout
In the church of Sant Felip Neri
And the aged woman in black is alert
To tabernacle gold, painted Christ's blood.

She touches images,
Her piety is a mantilla
Threadbare in this place;
Sanctuary lamp, gallows stare.

Swooped Hard

Swooped hard, wings intact
But could not land
Where Via Augusta
Becomes Plaza Molina.

The shimmering draught
Of one April evening;
No lasting city, and the affair
Ended in a green river.

Young Man with Doves

The young man with doves
Posing for a photo
In Plaça de Catalunya

Flashes a smile
That makes him young
Until he becomes a boy again.

Joy about the birds
Perched all over him
Makes him go back

To the blind source of all delight.

Virtual Flight Over the City

Heartache on day release:
Press to while away the time
Against the turnstile of memory.

The virtual tour skims milk of regret
Over the Bourbon-period buildings.

Soon we will look down
From the precipitous top of the zoom
At one of these spoken-for boulevards,
And see a face and remember.

Crepuscular

Sometimes, memory of indigo night
Or sense of the place without its skin,
Young lovers in a photo finish.

Crepuscular, pastel-tinted shrouds
Cloud the walls of Barrio Gótico.
Nightwalker, I wandered here

Players of viols and sackbuts
Chasing through the Gothic alleys
Typhoid in the drains, wormwood.

Dumb waiter, approach the city
By way of Albéniz, Granados, Tárrega
The lamenting of the choirs

Excavators of the remembered city.

Plaça Garrigues i Bachs

Plaça de la Seu, Sant Jaume,
Garrigues i Bachs, lovelorn places;
Now homeward, through the milky way

In the snow dark shimmer,
After all the sun today;
Run ragged, thin as a whip

After the comedown,
As though the strewn bed
Were in the streets.

The Summer Wind

Who would have resisted
Your bluebell eyes, flower dress,
Your fragrant presentiment.

Headily we were all heart
And cast our cautions
To the wind, but hesitant or not

We would be as chaff
In that summer wind.
Yet who would have resisted:

Even the trees could not hold back
Their leaves, waving scarecrow shadows
Where we walked.

II

Cornellà

I climbed and saw a great sight:
Norman Foster's communications tower
And the Temple del Sagrat Cor
On the summit of Tibidabo
Shimmering in the heat haze.

I have tried to find our casual ways again,
That Easter week of endless walking;
One year gone, and the merciless slide
Makes memory too a heat haze.

Municipal leaves of the city's trees
Have turned to lasting shadows;
All our happiness detonates
In these indelible streets.

Sant Tomàs

We came with twigs of instinct
Late in the season, tang of pine,

Whoop on the sand,
August cabaret of stars.

The colour plates are fading,
Our old daguerreotypes:

Another summer falling
And the place still calling.

Sevilla

The sound of midday bells
Brings a spirit so minded to Sevilla,
By the banks of the Guadalquivir.

We arose at five in the morning,
Set out through the sober land of Huelva
As day put on its spit and polish.

You were young enough
To kick a wild orange
Along the street and get away with it.

Carry These Lads Safe

Carry these lads safe:
Make the glad day
Of these young voyagers
Into golden fleece.

The bus in the shadows
And its precious cargo,
Moon low on the town
In the black early hours;

These argonauts and their quests —
Each life sacred, each journey.

Odd Days

I saw you odd days,
Nights, I walked under the plane trees
Avoiding the company,
Seeking out the locals, buoyant
With deflation, aigue and plague.

Prowled Gothic alleys, dark as mineshafts,
I saw green leaves shift
Chinese lantern-like
Against lights of inviting places,
I turned in dread and walked.

Avenida Diagonal ii

That April, in the vast city,
Don't want to say "once again"
Or on "a return visit"
Or anything over-arching

Those heavy oak doors
On Avenida Diagonal
Closing out the night,
Narrow stairs to narrow bed

And waking in the morning,
The city laying out its wares of light.

Preserve Integral

Preserve integral
Memory of that day

The young lovers
Stopping to buy flowers

The mayor ready to hand over
The keys to the city.

Silver Wings

Up the street here,
This side of brightness

Heart taken sideways
By the song about the little dove
With the silver wings.

Silvia Iriondo singing
And the sad piccolo guitar playing

Up the street here,
This side of brightness.

Old Cigar Smoke

Old cigar smoke is never the same again
But snow falls, its light beginnings
Unexpected across the Mediterranean city.

Huddled look of a Northern prefecture
Doomed by weather; snow falling, soundless,
Blackened in corners, staying for days.

La Basílica de Nuestra Señora de Begoña

I walk these steps rising
From the underbelly of the city,
In search of La Basílica
De Nuestra Señora de Begoña.

October's still sultry breath:
The few bars are lit way stations
Where talkers punch
The clock of the night.

I climb three steps a time;
Do not hear the returning sailors
Who said a *Salve Regina*
When they saw Begoña's steeple.

Smell of snuffed candles, wax,
Evaporated sin from between
The closed doors of La Basílica
De Nuestra Señora de Begoña.

I lose my way back.

When in That City

When in this or that Spanish city
I will customarily want to be
In that other one of memory;
There is a river like a rebuke in this one
And none in that sea-lapped place.

As if back in a forcing house
To renew what once stirred into being;
In truth any of these cities is an ice house,
You stoke long hours in its lethal flame
And on the cusp of midnight,
Tired of walking alone, feel the cold high point.

The Street of Eternal Memory

Green, translucent stamen brings
The true, torn spring, showers of light
Sloping from the surrounding hills.

In the blurry heat wave,
We have found, exhausted
A street called Carrer de l'Eterna Memòria

But sense too the undiscovered street
Running close to all the streets
We have known.

Barrio de Gracia

Hard lines, Sunday night
Stone in the mildewed fruit: Gracia
Of the ghosts, the fled companions.

Flower-sellers had others in mind today,
They sold well. Now on stony ground
Cold sober, you remember much

Too well like a reverse drunk;
Clarity like shards of hard ice
Resplendent in the sun.

III

Oncoming

The car brought them into the glare
Of an oncoming, spectral city;
The sodium lamps still idly on,
Murky brightness of a winter start.

The motorist was the father, the passengers
Were wife, or mother and their son:
The young blade and his cool haircut
The drool-light of dawn departing.

For father and son, a hereditary thing
Oncoming would take both early, not known
As yet in the course of that drive;
Pale explosions, headlights of oncoming cars

Might not be a city at all,
Light burrs and blurs,
Pesky brightness of a sharp morning
Or twilight, somewhere urban, diseased.

Mother's Dublin Train

You always said you wished you were that cow
Whisking flies with her tail from off her back
But the train moved on and the clatter over tracks

Rang the changes, relentlessly on to the city
Which duly presented dour steps of grime;
You followed upwards dutifully on time.

Did you take a laurel leaf from home,
Or from the walls a flake of lime?

News from America

for John Walsh

We drove the winding road
The tar melting, the car climbing
By dry stone walls, tussocky fields.

I was ten. Then you saw your marked man,
You could have closed one eye like an archer
To fix Jack Moroney in your sights

Where he worked the brow of a hill.
You parked the car, and I knew before
He knew what you were about to say:

Two men standing at some distance
From each other. I watched Jack
Lean on his pitchfork, suddenly blown

Into a dark corner, though unmoved
The cattle speechless; and I still know
More than Jack would ever know.

Paris Rain

All your minutes were hastening to their end
Though how were we to know,
Stuck in the rut of the afternoon
In the fin de siecle rain on Quai des Brumes.

We bought umbrellas, a red and a blue
In cafés you looked for the loo;
Age slowed you to small steps,
I raced on without a clue.

Rain was general over Notre Dame;
We argued over the tea and chips
You craved, eventually served
By a man in an upper room

Reached by a spiral stair:
Pommes frites and tea, the bill of fare
After our wear and tear, and the old rain
Pouring down the window pane.

Goat Path

On my own on the goat path,
Traffic endlessly declaiming,
Cars maddened by streets.

Remembering my arrival as seal pup
Wet behind the ears, flopping
On the dry land of lust

In the time of telex and sideburns;
Here I stand on the central median
Hearing the sound of the goat bell,

Wood chimes in my goat path.
Departed friend, sometimes sensed
The other side of a membrane

Thin as a spider's egg sac
In your hyena laughing heaven,
Our saturnine cackles in drinking places.

Evangelist of the pleasure of mere being,
You guided each and every traveller
You happened upon, on the goat path.

Seasons at Saint Peters

Desk-bound until half-past nine,
I ogled October through study-room glass;
Birds darted the dusk, sunset pouted
A carnival red mouth.

Opera singers down town sang delicious sin,
We had been warned; weak of spirit
Around the proscenium,
I longed for home.

February splayed flinty sun, I kept warm
At the samovar of a thought:
Easter would come and the outside
Open up the fields again.

News

The news came, father and I
Were stuck for words over breakfast
As the raven hovered in the garden.

Words and consolations, steam off cattle flanks;
Alone together in the kitchen,
In the stalled freeze-up.

The Widower's House

See him there, sitting in his yard
Staring at something; now he is up again,
Looking into a stall, carrying straw
Across mossed-over paving stones.

He is too far for me to read, but two daughters
Wave through the kitchen window,
Sound of water from the sink at which they stand
Like girls in Vermeer.

The garden seat is coming apart,
There are no roses in baskets, beds or buckets,
Nothing to say this season will soon end
And another begin.

Lines

Write here, on this yellowing
Unused receipt pad of yours
Headed with name and address
Whose blank, unfilled lines
Are silent about unsold things.

Write about other things
Besides the Sow River;
You didn't leave a paper trail,
Penned quick gags instead
Running riot on mother's letter head.

I see you writing between the lines
Of empty receipt, as mist
Wreathing morning pines
Writes in air, as ball bounces after,
As small whirlpools eddy.

The Outriders

in memoriam Seamus Heaney

They carried us here and there,
They smoked cigarettes
Whose brands have faded
But the outriders are mostly gone.

They jaunted us in cars between stone walls,
Gorse, ragwort, the cocks of hay we saved,
The empty floats we hitched a ride on.
Water where we played burst through

Under Moloney's Bridge and caught
The sun by its gills; dark bog-water
Turns bronze over the mottled stones,
But the outriders are mostly gone.

Castle Street

Alas poor Tom, tape measure
Around your shoulders, permanent cigarette
In mouth; mischief hid your secret tribulations
In light blasting summer display windows.

Time slid away, like a stream of old porter:
All the days you and father walked
Through Castle Street since you were
Brilliantined young men; walk-on parts
In the shops of friends, the years gone in mischief.

IV

Kassiopi

This go-by-the-wall and fly-by-night approach
Addicted to one city: remember you inside its ring
Like a fighter, you had to leave. What are you at,
Where are you going, and with what little grace?

Forked animal at the manicured fork in the road,
Your casual blur down the autopista
To catch the last breath of what you regard
As precious; or in another land entirely

Promenade in the heat of the day
By lamp shops, and the vendors of Greek statuary;
Your climbing high by Kalami, towards Kassiopi
In splashed lakes of sun and shadow

In the moving workshop of words,
Where turquoise waves break as crystal
On white granite: the prettiest place in the world,
Kassiopi, the prettiest place name.

Jade Sea

The jade sea before us, our days
Are beads of ice in the sun.
Greek dance under milk dust of stars:

What we want to remember
Wants to be remembered too
In a net whose fill empties

Through the ragged mesh of the years.

Every Asphalt Night

Every asphalt night,
Sky and pale stars

Slow stupor
Of the river in heat.

Here they all are, the heroes
Still breathing, have no doubt:

From across the water in Parga
You can take a boat trip to the River Styx.

Issos

The baking land talks
Forever it yaws on like thought,
The road ends at the strand.

I have been here, Issos,
The breeze winding through the olives,
Turning green leaves silver.

The quaking day,
A sun-burned martyr
Giving up its last.

Paxos

The pleasure boat eased down
The winding corridor of water
To Gaios, shadow fronds
On the harbour-front.

We walked a piece
On up the coast road
And lay in shallow water
Over a bed of prickly stones.

Paxos, toe end, memory add-on
Potency of the smaller thing become bigger:
Now comes melancholia's creaking hawser.

Moraitika

That time you went paragliding
In Moraitika and I travelled in the boat,
Quick with the nerve of the day.

Never further from your father
And never closer too
Up in the blue.

Chrysostomos

Over the morning wheat-fields
Crossing the Danube
Briefly melting the Alpine snow,
On the Sunday morning airwaves
The sung liturgy of Saint John Chrysostom.

Where dancers move
In Saturday night tavernas
To bouzouki music,
You will hear too
John the golden-mouthed.

The Road to Psarras

You were walking home that June night
Ahead of us, through velvet shadows
On the shore road.

Moon-mottled figure
Flapping in and out of flung light,
Trying to fill with hurried footsteps

The road under the olive trees:
Haunted, haunting, leaf upon leaf
Unknown to yourself, and we following.

Sidari

The sun so slayed us
That we could barely walk,
And we never saw the dunes

Sculpted by the wind, what matter.
So we waited at the bus stop
With the women in their preoccupations

Puff-balls, dust motes,
A rust curtain ballooning
In an open window

A tongue telling us to go back
From where we started
And begin again.

Olives are Waving

for Mary

Olives are waving
In the middle of the island;
The day will fall to marble stones
After the sieving of light.

Blue water will sleep,
Bright water bleed into darkness.

NOTES

EPIGRAPH
The opening epigraph is taken from Lawrence Durrell's translation
of Cavafy's poem, 'The City'.

VIBRANT GREY LIGHT
The epigraph is from the Italian *Si Dolce è'l Tormento,* lyrics by
Carlo Milanuzzi, music by Claudio Monteverdi, 1624. It translates
as follows:
So sweet is the torment
that lies in my breast,
that I live happily
because of its cruel beauty.

THE DESERTED BEACHES:
The epigraph to the poem features the opening lines of Antonio
Carlos Jobim's song in Portuguese, *As Praias Desertas.*

IN THE AMBER HUSH OF DUSK:
The line quoted is from *La Casita de Mis Viejos,* Spanish lyrics by
Enrique Cadicamo, music by Juan Carlos Cobían.

NO ONE THERE ON RETURN:
The duduk is a traditional Armenian woodwind instrument.